For

MOTHER'S LOVE

In Praise Of
African-American Mothers

Edited by Diane J. Johnson

PETER PAUPER PRESS, INC.
WHITE PLAINS, NEW YORK

Paintings by Synthia Saint James
Design by Arlene Greco

To Mommy, Nana, and Gran

Copyright © 1996
Peter Pauper Press, Inc.
202 Mamaroneck Avenue
White Plains, NY 10601
All rights reserved
Paintings copyright © 1991, 1992, 1993, 1995
Synthia Saint James
ISBN 0-88088-736-2
Printed in China
7 6 5 4

INTRODUCTION

Our mothers, grandmothers, and other women who have played a crucial role in shaping us are truly extraordinary. Our relationships with our mothers are born out of love, compassion, fear, gratitude, confusion, support, and occasional frustration. An indestructible bond grows out of the time that passes between mother and child. I am constantly struck with the gifts that have been provided to me by the love and commitment of my mother. Many are the unique lessons we learn from our African-American women who sacrifice, struggle, commit, and love us.

This book expresses the power of love that African-American women have for their children. It is a tribute to every African-American woman who has given of herself to raise a child.

D. J. J.

Paradise is open at the
command of mothers.

Egyptian Proverb

It was my mother who gave me my voice. She did this, I know now, by clearing a space where my words could fall, grow, then find their way to others.

Paula Giddings

I am my mother's, still, I am
very much my grandmother's
child. I was willed this sense
that your elders are your
gods on earth. I would have
walked behind my grand-
mother carrying an umbrella
if asked.

Lisa Jones

If you don't remember where you came from or how you got from there to here, you have a very hard time moving on. And you have to have goals to move from where you are.

Ada Deblanc Simonel

After I recorded it [*Plenty of Room*] and after I heard it a couple of times I realized that not only was this something that I was saying to my children, it was something that I wanted to hear my mother say to me.

Anita Baker

My mother once told me to stay humble, keep a smile on my face and watch how far I can go.

Teddy Riley

My mother is my root, my foundation. She planted the seed that I base my life on, and that is the belief that the ability to achieve starts in your mind.

Michael Jordan

I don't want Maya to be afraid to explore. And I want her to have the good fortune, and through the grace of God, to have a nucleus of good, loving and supportive people.

Victoria Rowell,
about her daughter

My mother gave us uncondi-
tional love, and *that* has been
invaluable in my work and
everyday life. Her love gives
me confidence and integrity.

Georgianna Robertson

She weeps for him a mother's
burning tears–
    She loved him with a
    mother's deepest love. . . .
        Paul Laurence Dunbar,
        Frederick Douglass

My dream for Savannah,
Kopper and Cheyenne is that
they will grow into beautiful
young women who love
themselves and therefore
don't need to be validated by
anyone else . . .

Jayne Kennedy Overton,
about her daughters

© '93 SYNTHIA SAINT JAMES

Only a baby, but strong
    and bright,
Making us happy from morn
    until night,
And knitting together with
    cords of love,
Those who were joined by
    the God above. . . .

N. F. Mossell,
    Only

A mother sat in the rosy dawn
    Of a morning bright
    and fair,
Her arms are round her first
    born son,
    Her breath is in his hair. . . .
                    N. F. Mossell,
                    Morning

Whatever you do, train a child up in the way of God, no matter what.

Whitney Houston

The source of [human] love
is of the mother.

African Proverb

You do your job and teach him. I'll do my job and see that his tuition gets paid.

Mother of Bruce Llewellyn,
African-American millionaire

I did it [raised my children] ad hoc, like any working mother does. Every woman who's got a household knows exactly what I did. I did it on a minute-to-minute basis. . . . There was never a place I worked, or a time I worked, that my children did not interrupt me, no matter how trivial–because it was never trivial to them.

Toni Morrison

One of my biggest dreams
for Lauren is that I am able
to teach her to be a secure,
strong and independent
woman who is capable of
taking care of herself, just as
my parents taught me.

Jody Watley,
about her daughter

I am the mother of sorrows,
I am the ender of grief; . . .
Paul Laurence Dunbar,
The Paradox

I have pushed hard against some of the rules of the "good daughter" and learned to really hear the message my mother has given me all my life: "I will be with you always." As in forever, into the eternal hereafter, no matter what.

Rebecca Walker,
daughter of Alice Walker

The doctors told me I would
never walk, but my mother
told me I would, so I
believed my mother.

Wilma Rudolph

There is no one who sympa-
thizes with us as much as
one's own mother; [for] who
is it will show kindness to
another person's child?

Yoruba Proverb

My grandmother often said,
"Learn to write . . . because it
is a piece of bread."

Yelena Khanga

Because when he was small, I knew more than he did, I expected to be his teacher. So because of him I educated myself. When he was 4, I started him to reading because I loved to read and he would interrupt when I was reading. So I taught him to read.

Maya Angelou

My mother always said,
"Make sure you get your
education, because they can
never take that away from
you."

Bill Bellamy

She knew she had us, and we were everything to her. So she sacrificed, and she worked hard, and she made it through.

Halle Berry,
about her mother

My dream for Ashley and Alexandra is to raise them to be all they can be, to nurture them into responsible, loving, secure, giving, human beings who not only find, but aren't afraid to go after, whatever it is that makes them happy in life.

Vanessa Bell Calloway

It's very hard to go to work
and not have guilty feelings. . . .
As a mother, you want to be
there to see their first steps,
hear their first words.

Sharon Johnson

We have to understand that we have the responsibility for being personally and mentally healthy ourselves in order to give our children what they need.

Dr. Grace Carroll Massey

Everyone asks how I find the
time for all the things I do. I
don't. I make the time. Being
a mother and a wife is
always demanding.

Florence Griffith Joyner

My mother, who is my spiritual touchstone, told me to remember three things in life: "You have one body, respect it; one mind, feed it well; and one life–enjoy it."

Des'ree

I had my son when I was twenty, and we grew up together. There never was this big authoritative thing where I felt that I had to lord over him the whole time. We were buddies.

Patricia Smith

I recognize that my mother, when she had me at 18, did what she knew how to do. I give her all the breaks in the world now. I am understanding that she was different then and did the best she knew how with a child in Mississippi in 1954.

Oprah Winfrey

If you can't hold them in
your arms, please hold them
in your heart.

Mother Hale

My mother is the major
tradition bearer in our family.
She told me the legends
before I was old enough to
go to school.

Kathryn L. Morgan

Black mothers have tradition-
ally drawn nourishment from
the rich heritage of Black
motherhood.

Peter J. Harris

I have a total of 22 years of absolute joy in having raised my children. I also have their hurts, their pain and their struggle—and that's what comes from sharing in the growth of that family. I've found my peace, and I've made it through.

Dr. Saundra Maass-Robinson

Mommy looked at me, her eyes squinched up in laughter, a grin spreading across her face. She loves for me to mess with her, gets a big kick out of my tongue-in-cheek assaults on her dignity. As if anything could ever put a dent in her dignity.

Bebe Moore Campbell

She said a long time ago,
"They spell my name
W-o-m-a-n." And that
means nobody takes
advantage of her.

Maya Angelou,
about her mother

My mother felt that I should
be a missionary nurse. Her
dream for me was to go
abroad to Africa and other
parts of the world to serve the
suffering. I have been something of a disappointment to
her ideal, but I think, from my
own view, I have done missionary work nonetheless.

Faye Wattleton

We were also vaguely taught
certain vague absolutes
[by our mother]: that we
were better than no one
but infinitely superior to
everyone . . .

Lorraine Hansberry

"Think of how you would like your children to remember you," [the artist] said earnestly. Still not thirty and not yet a mother, I found the request overly sentimental, and almost incomprehensible. I did, however, try to produce a look that conveyed goodness, nurturance, care, and understanding.

Sara Lawrence Lightfoot

As a parent you try to maintain a certain amount of control and so you have this tug of war . . . You have to learn when to let go. And that's not easy.

Aretha Franklin

I feel at peace in my heart and know that I have made peace with you, that you have forgiven me, and now we move in love, mother and daughter.

R. H. Douglas,
to her mother

Like all parents who reach a point of total frustration with the adolescent animal, my mother had taunted that she wished she could be a fly on the wall to see how I handled having a family.

Quo Vadis Gex-Breaux

Grandmother took me by the hand and said, "My child, let us pray." . . . On no other occasion has it been my lot to listen to so fervent a supplication for mercy and protection. It thrilled through my heart and inspired me with trust in God.

Harriet Jacobs,
Incidents from a Slave Girl

I was Grandma's namesake. . . . She had marked me, she said, with a mole just above my upper right lip. She had one in the same spot, so that as much as justified her insistence that I bear her name.

Deborah E. McDowell

I had very strong women role models in my mother, my grandmother, and my aunt. They used to say, "When you fall down, get up. If you fall down again, get up. And don't be ashamed of falling down."

Carrie Saxon Perry

At this point in my life I think that I have put my grandmother's ways into perspective and have come to appreciate many of the things she taught me. Besides usable skills like sewing, she taught me self-discipline, which is very important.

Barbara Smith

I dig being a mother . . . and of course, as a grandmother, I just run amok.

Whoopi Goldberg

My mother sang with me in her stomach; I sang with Bobbi Kris in my stomach. I believe the child starts to develop within, and whatever is put inside of you–whatever you read, whatever you think, whatever you do– affects the child.

Whitney Houston

My strongest, and fondest,
memories from childhood
center on listening to my
mother sing. All day and all
night . . . she was carrying a
song . . .

Anthony Walton

Anything that happens, you can confide in Mama. Mama loves each child the way God loves His children. Nothing's too bad to tell Mama. Don't ever tell me a lie. It's not necessary, because Mama will understand.

Nanny James Logan Delany,
mother of the Delany sisters

I turn to look at my mother
and she looks back at me.
She knows my thoughts well,
because they are very similar
to her own. She has been
thinking about the dreams
I sometimes hear her
dreaming . . .

Natasha Tarpley

I don't think Mama would have been at all surprised that Sadie and I have kept living this long. We learned a lot from her about being old. Mama set a good example.

A. Elizabeth "Bessie" Delany

I always thought of her as big because of the things that she did; I just visualized her as being real tall and big, but this was not true. My mother was shorter than I am, and Harriet Tubman was about five feet one inch or five feet one and a half inches tall.

Mariline Wilkins,
great-grandniece of Harriet Tubman,
speaking of her from stories
told by her mother

My mother always said you can do whatever you want to. She always went after whatever she wanted, and instilled that in me. She's very strong, very opinionated, never holds back. I'm strong, but I don't think I'm as strong as my mom.

Vanessa Williams

You're a great mom and I
love you. I'm outta here.

Michael Boyd,
son of Julia Boyd

My mom always taught us that family's all you have when everything's said and done. You have to love them and support them no matter who they are, no matter how they look, no matter how they may behave.

Toni Braxton

O ye mothers, what a responsibility rests on you! It is you that must create in the minds of your little girls and boys a thirst for knowledge, the love of virtue, . . . and the cultivation of the pure heart.

Maria Stewart

I like to think of my literary voice as my "mother language." To a great extent, that voice is indeed my mother's voice.

Tina McElroy Ansa

My father grabbed life by the arm and wrestled it into squealing submission. My mother cleared the same terrain with a faith and self-possession that both fueled and ruined some of her dreams.

Marita Golden

Every day that I'm here, I try
to be worthy of the kind of
person my mother wanted
me to be.

Ruth Simmons,
president of Smith College

As I watch my mother . . . I can feel the peacefulness that she emanates, but I also know that inside she is nervous with anticipation. . . . She believes in "the Word" and hopes to communicate, not merely entertain or fill time . . .

Sara Lawrence Lightfoot

I have a child who is 4 years old, and, of course, I want to say his IQ is off the boards. But if that IQ measurement doesn't measure how he is going to contribute to his society, it means nothing.

Gail Wright Sirmans

A mother is not to be
compared with another
person–she is incomparable.
African Proverb